Creepy Creatures

Set 2

Fireflies

Nancy Dickmann

Chicago, Illinois

© 2006 Raintree
Published by Raintree, a division of Reed Elsevier, Inc.
Chicago, Illinois
Customer Service 888-363-4266
Visit our website at www.raintreelibrary.com

Printed and bound by South China Printing Company.
10 09 08 07 06
10 9 8 7 6 5 4 3 2 1

Library of Congress Cataloging-in-Publication Data:
Dickmann, Nancy.
   Fireflies / Nancy Dickmann.
      p. cm. -- (Creepy creatures)
   Includes index.
   ISBN 1-4109-1770-3 (library binding - hardcover) -- ISBN 1-4109-1775-4 (pbk.)
   1. Fireflies--Juvenile literature. I. Title. II. Series.

QL596.L28D53 2006
595.76'44--dc22

                                        2005012453

Acknowledgments
The publishers would like to thank the following for permission to reproduce photographs:: Alamy Images pp. **4**, **5**, **8** (Phil Degginger), **12–13** (AM Corporation); Coris p. **21**; Cornell University News Service p. **20** (Thomas Eisner); Nature Picture Library p. **23** (Barry Mansell); Oxford Scientific Films pp. **10** (Animals Animals), **11** (James H Robinson), **18**, **19** (Animals Animals/James E Lloyd), **23** (Animals Animals/James E Lloyd); Oxford Scientific Films/Satoshi Kuribayashi pp. **6–7**, **14**, **15**, **16–17**, **22**; P D Pratt p. **9**.

Cover picture of a firefly reproduced with permission of Dwight Kuhn.

Every effort has been made to contact copyright holders of any material reproduced in this book.
Any omissions will be rectified in subsequent printings if notice is given to the publishers.

Some words are shown in bold, **like this**. You can find out what they mean by looking in the glossary on page 24.

2

Contents

Fireflies

Fireflies are small insects.

They have flashing lights on their **abdomens.**

Sometimes we call them "lightning bugs."

Looking for Fireflies

You can see fireflies flying at **dusk**.

6

You might see young fireflies glowing on the grass.

A Firefly's Body

Fireflies are dark with bright markings.

two antennae

two pairs
of wings

They have two **antennae** and two pairs of wings.

A firefly has a special section on its **abdomen**.

It glows with a
special light.

Meeting Up

A male firefly flashes his light.

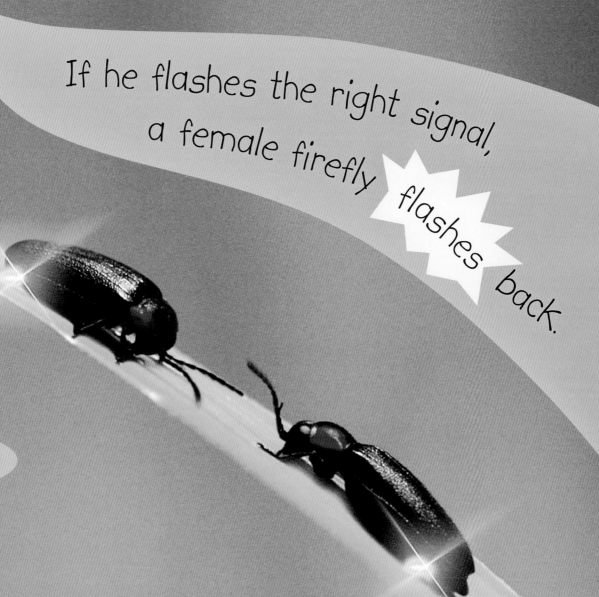

If he flashes the right signal, a female firefly flashes back.

Firefly Eggs

The female firefly lays lots of little eggs.

Sometimes the eggs glow.
Young fireflies **hatch** out of the eggs.

Young Fireflies

All young fireflies glow.
They crawl like worms.

We call them
"glowworms."

Food for Fireflies

Glowworms eat snails and worms.

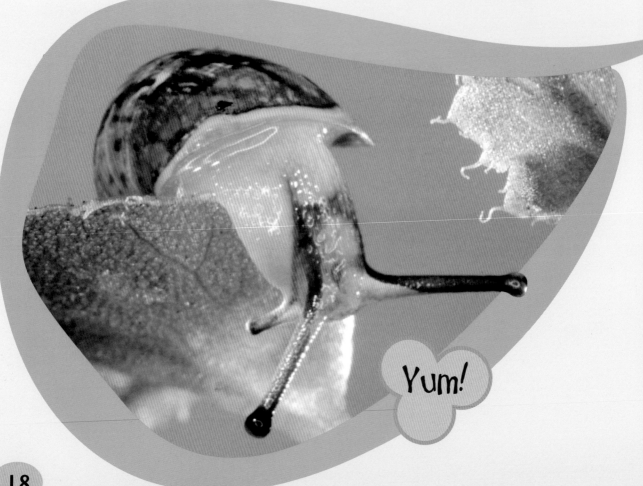

Yum!

Fireflies feed on plants.

Fireflies in Danger

Birds, lizards, and spiders eat fireflies.

Some frogs eat so many they start to glow!

Types of Fireflies

There are hundreds of different kinds of fireflies.

They live all over the world.

Glossary

abdomen middle of the body

antenna (More than one are antennae.) feeler on an insect's head that helps it smell, see, or hear

dusk in the evening before it is night

hatch to come out of an egg

Index

Notes for Adults

This series supports the young child's exploration of their learning environment and their knowledge and understanding of their world. Using the books in the series together will enable comparison of similarities and differences to be made. (NB. Many of the photographs in **Creepy Creatures** show them much larger than life size. The first spread of each title shows the creature at approximately its real life size.)

This book introduces the reader to the life cycle and behavior of the firefly. It will also help children extend their vocabulary as they hear new words like *abdomen*, *antennae*, and *dusk*. You may like to introduce and explain other new words yourself, like *habitat*, *larva*, and *species*.

Additional Information

Fireflies are a type of small beetle, about 5 to 20 mm long. Most are dull brown or black, with red, orange, or yellow markings. They have two pairs of wings, but only one is used for flying. Females are often wingless. A chemical reaction takes place in special light organs on the abdomen to produce light without heat. Fireflies use their light to find a mate; they are usually most active in early evening. The female lays eggs on moist ground; the eggs of some species give off light. The eggs hatch into glowing, flightless larvae. Adults live at most one month, and some eat nothing during this time. There are about 1,900 species in all, found on every continent except Antarctica.

Follow-up Activities

• Fireflies signal to each other with flashing light. Can the children think of other ways that animals or insects communicate with each other?
• Draw, paint, or make models of fireflies.
• Read a fictional story such as *Firefly Friend* by Kimberly Klier, and ask the children to relate the events to factual information in this book.

24